Mother Love

A One Act Play

Catrina J. Sparkman

ISBN 13: 978-1-949958-14-0

Mother Love Copyright © 1996 Catrina J. Sparkman

Published in 2015 by:

The Ironer's Press
PO Box 1122
Madison, Wi 53701

SOFTCOVER EDTION
ISBN 13: 978-1-949958-14-0

All rights reserved. No part of this book may be reproduced, stored in whole or in part or transmitted in any form by any means, without prior written permission from the publisher, except in the case of brief quotations embodied in articles for review. Nor can this book be circulated in any form of binding or cover other than that in which it is published.

This is a work of fiction. Any reference or similarities to actual events, real people, living or dead, or to real locales are intended to give the novel a sense of reality. Any similarity in other names, characters, places and incidents is entirely coincidental.

Obtaining the Stage Production Rights for *Mother Love*:

Please note, this is not a public domain work. Your purchase of this play in any format, digital or physical, does not entitle you to the right to stage the play in any type of production. To obtain the performance and or production rights of this copyrighted material, please contact The Ironer's Press on behalf of the author and copyright holder, Catrina J. Sparkman

Other Works by Catrina J. Sparkman

Plays

Territory

The Cinderella Show

The Gospel According to Ruth
(screenplay)

Non-fiction

Doing Business with God: An Everyday Guide to Prayer & Journaling

Intimacy the Beginning of Authority

Divine Revelation for a Twitter Generation

Fiction
Passing Through Water
Opening the Floodgates
The Fire This Time

Production History

Mother Love was first produced on March 4, 1996 at the Frederic March Play Circle Theater

The play was directed by Darrell Allbriton, Jr.

The role of Bebina Moore was played by Renita Evans and Precious Robinson.

The role of Belinda Moore was played by Nicole Anderson.

The role of Celess Moore was played by Lori Woodall.

Author's Note

Mother Love holds a special place in my heart because it is the first play that I had ever written that had been produced. I wrote *Mother Love* during a very tumultuous time in my own life, were much like the character Celess, I had to take a good introspective look at my past. During those days of self-reflection and recalled memory I can remember shedding a whole lot of tears and a whole lot of pain. It was amidst the tears, the introspection, and the purging that ***Mother Love*** was born.

As I wrote about the Moore family, I was able to safely examine my own story. As I told their story, I discovered an impenetrable truth about my identity. What I am not is a mere expression of what has occurred in the past. What I am is so much greater than my experiences. This play *Mother Love* is so dear to me because it birthed my own personal healing and it helped me find my voice.

It is my prayer that as you read this or listen to it if that be the case that you will find among the pages healing, forgiveness, personal agency and most importantly, voice.

—Catrina J. Sparkman

Cast of Characters

Bebina Moore -age 69, African American, the former first lady of Ebenezer Baptist Church. She is mother to Belinda Moore, grandmother to Celess Thomas. Bebina speaks her lines from her living room parlor in **Little Rock, Arkansas**, her audience is God.

Belinda Moore – age 53, African American, an alcoholic and washed out jazz singer, mother of Celess Thomas. She speaks her lines on stage at a nightclub in **LA** to a near empty room.

Celess Thomas- age 38, African American. She is a child psychologist speaking from her office in **Atlanta.** She is recording her memoirs.

Soloist- The singer is planted in the crowd who stands and sings *Motherless Child* at a point in the script the director chooses

Production Notes

Mother Love tells the story of the Moore family, a family composed of three generations of African American women. Each of the Moore women appear on stage simultaneously and speak their lines from three different parts of the country: Celess, the youngest member, is a child psychologist who speaks her lines from Atlanta. Bebina Moore, the 69 year old matriarch of the family speaks her lines from Little Rock, Arkansas. Belinda Moore, a 53 year old jazz singer and alcoholic, speaks her lines from up on stage, to a nearly empty room in a nightclub in LA.

As the story unfolds, we see that it is more than geography that separates this family. They have been separated by a history of abuse and violence. Celess has been raped. When her mother, Belinda Moore, finds out she commands the eight year old never to speak of the incident again. Instead she puts her on a bus to Little Rock, Arkansas. She sends her away to live with her mother, Bebina Moore, who she refers to as "the pillar of strength." Thirty years later when the play opens, each of these women is grappling with the ramifications of years of silence. This is a story about restoration, and forgiveness. A story about the need to find one's own voice and use it.

The three women appear on stage together, each unaware of the other's presence. While speaking her lines each woman is illuminated while the other two remain frozen in time in the shadows.

Belinda Moore is seated (stage left) on a bar stool. There is a microphone in front of her, as well as a bottle of vodka. When the lights come up a neon sign is flashing behind her with the name of the club [director's choice] and the city, Los Angeles, California.

She is dressed in tight black leather pants, a white tube top, a red leather jacket, heels, and way too much make-up. She has a white gardenia flower in her hair like that worn by her idol the late and tragic Billy Holiday. Belinda stage direction notes that she is drinking. In fact she is a 'happy drunk' at the start of the play on her way to becoming a sloppy drunk as the play progresses. She staggers on stage, caressing her Vodka bottle as if it were a child.

Bebina Moore is seated in her parlor (center stage). Bebina's parlor is that of a southern family of considerable means. There should be a window she could look out and an upright piano. Framed newspaper articles from the *Arkansas Gazette* and the *Little Rock Daily* are blown up and hang from the wall above the piano in honor of her late husband Rev. Ezekiel Moore. The articles signify her devotion to him and also serve as a location marker to the audience. Bebina is a well dressed, meticulously groomed woman, the antithesis of her daughter Belinda. Being a very spiritual woman most of her lines are spoken as prayers to God. At one point, her stage direction says she is watching. Watching is a spiritual code which means to pray with fervor as well as increased understanding.

Celess Thomas is in her Atlanta office (stage right). Her office looks like the typical psychologist office. Adorned with a desk, bookcase and couch, knick knacks are scattered through out the room. There is a plant as well as a small box of toys for clients to interact with. Among the toys is a truck as well as several African American rag dolls. A framed poster of the Chicago skyline with the caption *Chicago the Windy City* hanging over her desk. Celess is your average well dressed professional. She is meticulously groomed, like her grandmother. Her stage direction [running] is not a physical running but symbolic running. Running represents Celess never facing or dealing with her childhood. She often paces around her office as she speaks her lines into a small recorder. Stopping and starting over again. She is recording her memoirs. When she is [still] she is coming to grips with her horrific past and the ramifications of her rape.

BELINDA

[*Drinking*] My mama hates me. Course she wouldn't say so, being so well respected in our town and all. Wouldn't look right to hate her own kin, but she does. Has ever since my Daddy died.

CELESS

[*Running*] I just wish growing up that I would have had someone to hold me, to love me, to tell me that everything would be all right. I never felt that way until I met my husband Jubul—that bothers me. The fact that I could be 35 years old and starved for love.

BELINDA

She just jealous cause he loved me more than he loved her. I know that's what it is. She jealous. My Daddy use to hold me, and rock me and play with me. He'd say I was the prettiest thing surely ever born. And what did he say to her? He just looked at her like she wasn't even there.

BEBINA

[*Praying*] I knew Belinda was Zeek's child when she wouldn't take my milk. I thought something was wrong with my baby, until the doctor told me to try her on formula for a few days. And it worked, she ate just fine.

BELINDA

Everybody in our town loved my Daddy, Ezekiel Moore! He was the pastor of our church, and folk would come from miles around to get slayed in the spirit, cause my daddy sure could preach. Some folk say he could make the devil shout!

BEBINA

I cried and carried on about something being wrong with my baby. Belinda was crying something fierce too, until I put that artificial nipple in her mouth, and fed her that powdered milk. Zeek laughed at me and said, "Woman, who do you think want to drink from your old wrinkled up tittes?"

BELINDA

When I was a young girl I usta sing in church every Sunday, and when I had a solo, not a dry eye would be in the place. My Daddy would be in the pulpit about to burst with pride, his little girl up there singing for the Lord. I never sang for the Lord though, never once, I always sang for my Daddy. Nobody ever knew it.

CELESS

I never knew my father. In fact, I don't think my mother really did either. When I was a little girl and I use to ask about my Daddy she'd say:

BELINDA

The stork brought you. You ain't got no dadd

CELESS

Imagine my embarrassment when my third grade teacher asked us to talk about our parents, who they were and what they did for a living. I live with my mother Belinda Moore. I say assertively. She's a housewife. 'Oh?' said Ms Smith, 'What does your father do, Celess?' 'I don't have a father, I was brought by the stork,' I say with equal assertion. Maybe the absurdity of that statement said with such conviction was what made them laugh, 'Well, Celess,' said Ms. Smith, trying to save face, hers and mine, 'Not everyone lives with their real daddy. Some daddies have died or they just can't get along with the mommies. What does your step-daddy do?' I wasn't prepared for that. It never occurred to me that in order to be a housewife you

CELESS (CONT.)

needed to have a husband. I had already used the bulk of my brain power to give Belinda a normal life. Now I was expected to turn water into wine. I mean I couldn't tell the truth, 'My mother is an unemployed jazz singer, she's in between gigs right now and we live off government aid.' My brain swirled through a list of faces like a carousel—A caravan of men who could be seen gallivanting through our apartment on any given night. The carousel stopped on a picture of Mick, a white man we knew, and I lied.

BEBINA

Looking back, I realized I spent my whole life living inside that man. I don't remember anything about my life really, outside of

BEBINA (CONT.)

Zeek, except my mama. I think of her every now and again. I guess if I think hard enough I could remember what it was like to be young, but even then Zeek made sure I didn't feel it. He needed to be in control of that feeling too. And me, like a fool, I let him.

Of course I was jealous, some mothers would never think it, but I'm not afraid to, Lord. Zeek's smile was the sun. He could look at you, flash those big pearly whites, and make your whole lonely inside light up. Make everything in you dead come alive again. I lived inside of that smile. I was like that old oak tree out front, protecting this house for over 50 years, hiding the hurt and the pain. I was the prefect minister's wife. I painted a picture perfect setting that other women

BEBINA (CONT.)

envied. I lived my life in seasons, always waiting for the sun. Nobody but God protects the trees.

BELINDA

[*drinking harder*] And he was fine, so very, very, fine. Everybody said so! He was fine and black, a silky, purple, blue, smooth, kind of Black. That's the kind of handsome my daddy was.

BEBINA

I lived my life in seasons always waiting for the sun.

CELESS

Mystepdaddyisatruckdriver. I say. 'I'm sorry Celess, everyone in the class can't hear you.' He's a truck driver. I repeat. Some of the boys in my class look impressed. Ms. Smith looks relieved, some of the redness seems to dissipate from her face, and me, I was just thankful for my black skin.

BELINDA

He was fine and Black, a silky-purple-blue-smooth-kind of Black!

BEBINA

I painted a picture perfect setting that other women envied.

CELESS

I was just thankful for my black skin.

BEBINA

It was cold in his shadow, my roots never expanded, they just twisted and turned around themselves, until they threatened to choke themselves. He never seemed to let me die though, which is what I sometimes wanted to do. I realize now, that he needed me there to want his love. He couldn't let me die. So he would smile one of those big ole smiles that lighted up the whole world, and for a minute, I would live again. I lived for a lifetime off of that smile, never flourishing,

BEBINA (CONT.)

only sustaining, off of a smile, or a compliment. 'B,' he'd tell me, 'You looking mighty fine in that dress.' Or, 'Wear the red one B, it looks good on you.' It was like rain after a drought. And it kept me until he died. Then my anger kept me, and I flourished, strong, tall, proud, and free—or so I thought.

BELINDA

Seems like on the very day my Daddy died she changed. Seems like meanness musta been crouching in her soul, and when he died it rose up and began walking around in her place. Living out her hatred for him. Oh she did all of her wifely duties, honored his memory, never even looked at another man. Although she was

BELINDA (CONT.)

still real pretty. She was the prefect widow. Privately, I think she hated him. Yes, it became clear to me she hated him and me. I can understand her being angry with him, any woman would have, but why she have to hate me? I was her child.

BEBINA

I look out my big bay window everyday and I think sometimes about the first day Zeek brought me to this place. I wasn't but sixteen years old and green as a Mississippi summer. I looked at that tree and I said now you've got to teach me, because I don't know. She has been teaching me every since.

BELINDA

By the time I was thirteen I had declared a quiet war against my mother. She was beautiful, so beautiful that when she walked into a room she would take your breathe away. I was confused. I didn't know whether I should love her and be proud of her perfection or if I should hate her and be envious. Love is a complicated emotion when you thirteen. Hate is faster, easier.

CELESS

When I was a little girl I was raped

BEBINA

Of course I was jealous of her. I was jealous of him too. They both seemed to stand where I was

BEBINA (CONT.)

supposed to. 'Babe' he'd say, 'I think I'm going to sleep in Belinda's room tonight, she's afraid of the dark.' 'Zeek,' I'd say, real amicable and nice like, 'Belinda's a little girl, it's not fitting for her to sleep in the same room as her daddy, even if he is sleeping on the fold-out cot.' Then she would throw a fit like a little white child and Zeek would give Belinda her way. Didn't I go to my mother when I was afraid?

BELINDA

I did some evil things to my mother to try to hurt her. Foolish things that children do when they young and mad. I would ask the women in the church to sew things for me, even though I knew my mama was the best seamstress in

BELINDA (CONT.)

town. I wanted to make her feel as incompetent as she made me. I looked for a certain kind of woman to aid me in my plan. I'd search out the ones that looked up from the pews just dripping with desire for my daddy, the ones that had enough sugar in their voices to kill a diabetic, and the ones with a switch in their behinds that could hypnotize the blind. The ones my mama and the elders of the church called:

ALL

Jezebel!

BELINDA

I'd corner them after service in the back of the church and began talking about how good I thought their daughter's looked that

BELINDA (CONT.)

Sunday. I'd swear up and down that those raggedy dresses they wore looked better then outfits I'd seen in fashion magazines. Sometimes I'd throw in something real clever like, how I wish my mama had their sense of style. Them hot breeches would fly home to them machines, yank that cheap material off their girls backs and get ready to set Pastor Zeek's daughter out real fine! My mama wouldn't be phased though, not one bit. When they'd get to our house she'd be waiting for them. She'd tell them real nice like:

BEBINA

Thank you Ms. Jackson, Sister Merriweather, for your concern, but Belinda has a closet full of

BEBINA (CONT.)

beautiful clothes, more clothes than any 13 year old child has need or time to wear. I took the liberty of composing for you a list of some of the more needy families in our community, I can call them for you if you like, to let them know that you'll be on your way.

BELINDA

[*Laughing.*] She sure would tell them! Then afterwards she'd look at me and read me too.

BEBINA / BELINDA

Belinda, you not fooling nobody. I know you didn't want that tired dress!

BEBINA

That tree taught me patience. It taught me how to hold my peace and be still. Yes Lord, that tree taught me everything I know. For 48 years now I've watched that tree live and die. I watched it in the winter when it was cold and bare. I watched the growing pains of the spring, and I watched autumn come and that old oak loose all her hair. I learned a lot from that old tree. Yes Lord, I learned how to live and die gracefully.

CELESS

[*Running faster*] When I was a little girl I was raped. When I was a little girl I was raped. When I was a little girl I was raped.

BEBINA

[*Watching*] I had a beautiful relationship with my mother when I was a little girl. I wish me and my daughter could have had the same. I feel like I failed. I feel like I taught her by my example. And if my example taught her nothing else, Lord, it taught her that I sure did love my man. By teaching her how to love my man, did I teach her how to hate herself? Lord, seems like all this time that's all I been doing is hating myself. Seems like when she left home Belinda proved she didn't have love for nobody but Zeek, not even herself. Sleeping around with first one man then the next. I knew it was her father's love she was looking to recreate even if only for a moment. And all I could think about was how different we were, but I see now that we weren't that different after all. We just at two

BEBINA (CONT.)

opposite sides of the spectrum, both trying to make the rainbow. Belinda giving her love to everybody. Me, not giving my love to anybody, not even my own child. The first time I saw her going down that road of destruction I tried to warn her! I would be on her like white on rice telling her, 'Belinda, you've got to have some respect about yourself!' But criticism from the one you believe does not love you sounds cruel- and maybe it was, because pain had sucked all of the softness out of me and only the fierceness of my love remained. You never stop loving your children just sometimes to them, it don't feel like love.

BELINDA

[*Sobering, she lowers herself to the floor.*] I had a baby when I was fourteen. She looks a lot like me. When I first held her in my arms and saw her face I thought for once in my life that my daddy was wrong, cause she was definitely the most beautiful thing in all the world—far more prettier than me. Real refined too. Just like my mama. She's a child psychologist. That's right, a professional and she come out of me. She always wanted to call me mama, I never let her though. I was just a baby myself, I wasn't ready to be nobody's mama. A sister, now that was something I could be. I was her big sister, because a big sister was what I always wanted and I thought that Celess would want one too. But she wanted what all little girl's want, a mama. When she was a real little girl she

BELINDA (CONT.)

would sit on the couch beside me and brush my hair.

CELESS

Celess lowers herself to the floor and begins to brush a rag doll's hair.

BELINDA

I like that, the way her soft little hands felt in my hair. She'd be sitting there brushing my hair and she'd ask me in that small little high pitched voice.

CELESS

B'linde can I call you mama? Please? Only when it's me and you.

BELINDA

I wouldn't say nothing. I'd just kinda pull away, and sit there, scared halfway out my mind at the thought of being somebody's mama. I don't think she ever really got over not having a mother.

CELESS

[*Still.*] When he called me over to his truck, I thought nothing of it. After all, he was my surrogate stepfather. At least that's what I had told my class. Besides, he'd been over our house many evenings playing cards and

CELESS (CONT.)

drinking beer with Belinda. And late at night, when Belinda thought I was asleep, they would go into the back room and make the bed rattle. All the kids in school said their mommies and daddies made the bed rattle. It made sense to me that my surrogate dad would not hurt me. He wasn't a stranger. For a brief moment when I told her I thought I saw something in her face like love-fear-concern or at least guilt. A medley of emotions seemed to fly across her face, none of them fully distinguishable to me. Just for a moment. Then the old Belinda returned.

BELINDA

[*scrambles up quickly from the floor*] All girl, I thought you done got killed or something! You out

BELINDA (CONT.)

her being a crybaby. Look a here, he done did you a favor. Some little boy was bound to come around here sooner or later and bust your cherry. Now it ain't gonna hurt none when he do. I wasn't no older than you when it happened to me!

CELESS

IT HURTS!!!!!

BELINDA

Belinda covers her ears to drown out the sound.

BELINDA/ CELESS

Get use to it girl cause it's what mens want, and if you ever going to keep a man, you're gonna have to give him what he wants. Now it hurt the first time but it feel good each additional time. Go in the house. Wash up, stop all that crying and I'll buy you some candy. Don't you ever tell anybody about this.

CELESS

We never spoke again of the rape.

BELINDA

Sometimes in my sleep I hear Celess scream. I see her running to me as she did that day with blood streaming down her legs. I wake up in a cold sweat and only a

BELINDA (CONT.)

stiff drink can make me forget. I tried to play it off when it happened. I tried to make it seem like what happened to her wasn't no big deal. That way she wouldn't be traumatized. Then I went to the gun shop and bought me a .45 and I went looking for Micky. First I blew his penis off and watched him as he crawled around looking for his organ, begging and sloshing, and begging in all that blood. I thought of my Daddy and I asked his forgiveness as I pulled the trigger again and blew his brains out. Nobody ever found out what I did. It took fifteen minutes. For fifteen minutes I was a mother.

CELESS

I love to hear the word mama fall from my children's sweet lips. I

CELESS (CONT.)

always wanted to call my mother mama, but she would never permit it. She would tell me to call her by her given name that way people would think we were sisters. Men didn't want to be bothered with women with babies. One day I almost hit my daughter for calling me Celess. It's just a phase that some children go through—wanting to call their parents by their given names. Jubul just laughed when she called him by his name and said, 'Yes, what can I do for you, Miss Tasha Ann?' All playful like. I had to resist slapping her, so instead I spoke through clenched teeth, 'Don't call me that, honey. Call me mama or mommy.' All along my hand itched to slap her face. Sometimes the love I have for my kids seems so terrible; dysfunctional even.

CELESS (CONT.)

Sometimes I feel like I want to squeeze the life out of them, gobble them up whole, and keep them deep within my belly, so they will never have the chance to be hurt, always protected by me.

BELINDA

So I sent her away so she could never be hurt again. I bought her a ticket and I sent her back to Arkansas. I sent her to my mother the pillar of strength. It was my second act as a mother.

CELESS

My grandmother is a formidable woman. She's a good woman, an admirable woman, but Lord knows

CELESS (CONT.)

she doesn't know much about expressing love. Looking through adult eyes, I can see that she'd been hurt and that hurt caused her to give the people in her life the essentials without love. She gave me food, shelter, a good education, formal training, good morals and values, but I can count the times my grandmother gave me a hug. Once, at a banquet when they nominated her Woman of the Year. I was called upon to present her the award. I think now even that was for public appearance. Growing up, I called her grandmother not per her request, but because her demeanor seemed to not permit anything less. Grandma or granny just would not do. I felt like I repulsed her. I felt like she took care of me because it was her duty and that alone. Sometimes I wonder about her.

CELESS (CONT.)

What did she live through that made her such a shell? Only God knows my daily prayer, that the unsaid things about or family's history one day be said.

BEBINA

And yes Lord, I know now that you gave me a second chance with my granddaughter, but I pushed her away too. Truth is she reminded me of myself. Seems like Celess was just like me, she didn't have a place. Belinda didn't want her no more than she or Zeek had wanted me. She was simply there to protect. Sometimes I'd get a feeling in the middle of the night that my child was in danger. My heart would go to beating really fast and I would see my granddaughter's face. I wouldn't

BEBINA (CONT.)

know what city they were in at the time cause Belinda was always on the road, singing that jazz, moving around to different places; but when I saw Celess' face, I knew in my spirit that they would be alright. That little girl was an angel. She was a tree her mother could lean on. I don't know how she survived herself, cept only God protects the trees.

CELESS

I always wanted to ask her why she gave me away. Why she sent me to live with my grandmother after Micky. I never did. It never seemed like the right moment. Conversations with Belinda are always so full of laughs and jokes. 'We laugh to keep from crying,' someone once said. I laugh

CELESS (CONT.)

because I learned a long time ago that tears were not acceptable to my mother.

BELINDA

The worst thing I ever did was tell her to keep quiet. I should have let her scream from the rooftop what that bastard did to her. Instead I told her to be quiet. We never talked about the rape. I kept that .45 though, it reminds me of love. I kept that .45. I kept that .45

BEBINA

Only the fierceness of my love remained.

CELESS

I feel like I want to squeeze them, swallow them up whole…

BELINDA

I kept that .45.

CELESS

Keep them deep within my belly. Never to be hurt, always protected by me.

BELINDA

I kept that .45 it reminds me of love.

BEBINA

My daughter called me today, drunk out of her mind and crying.

BEBINA (CONT.)

She said that years ago my granddaughter was raped, and that she had killed the man who did it. For almost 30 years now the demons of the past have tormented her. As I hung up the phone I realized it was the first time we had ever talked. And Father, forgive me, but when she told me what she had done, I was proud.

BELINDA

Mama, I need help.

BEBINA

We'll get you some.

BELINDA

Mama, am I going to hell?

BEBINA

I don't think so baby. Belinda?

BELINDA

Yes, Mama?

BEBINA

I would have done the same thing.

BELINDA

I knew she was talking about me. Maybe, God, my mama don't hate me. No, God, I know my mama don't hate me. Maybe she ain't

BELINDA (CONT.)

always liked my ways, and I ain't always liked hers, but she don't hate me. I knew what she meant. The moment I pulled that trigger I understood mother love. It's explosive, it's fierce. At that moment I didn't care about the consequence, I only knew that my child was hurting and that a life was required. When it was done I only felt love. It may be lacking a whole lot but it's still love.

CELESS

My mother has a problem, she been drinking now for years and nobody knew it. We are checking her into a drug and alcohol rehabilitation program this week. She started drinking after the rape. My grandmother says to keep the voices away. I'm flying out to

CELESS (CONT.)

Little Rock tomorrow. [*Celess moves downstage and joins hands with Bebina.*] My grandmother and I are flying to Los Angeles.

Bebina and Celess both walk towards and join hands with Belinda

CELESS

From there we will all drive down to Minnesota. My colleagues tell me of a place there that has one of the best rehabilitation programs in the country. It's a long drive, there will be plenty of time to talk. God does answer prayer.

BELINDA

I kept that .45 it reminds me of love.

BEBINA

Lord, forgive me but when she told me what she'd done, I was proud.

BELINDA

[*Speaking to Celess.*] We never talked about the rape.

CELESS

[*Speaking to Belinda.*] We never talked about the rape.

BEBINA

[*Speaking to Belinda and Celess.*]
We never talked.

ALL

Until now.